IN MY CAPACITY: I LOVE AND SURRENDER

PALAK AAROHI

Made with ♥ on the Notion Press Platform
www.notionpress.com

I dedicate this book to all the readers.

More power to you!

This book is also dedicated to my parents, Love you!

Contents

JUST QUESTIONS

YOU MADE USE OF ME TO FILL THE EMPTINESS

THAT WAS INSIDE YOU.

WHY NOT ME

WHAT UNITES US ALL?

THE UNCOMFORTABLE TRUTH

NOT EVEN MINE

THE SPARK IS GONE

Read It Out Loud

ANSWER TO ALL THE QUESTIONS

FOR THE PEOPLE WHO HAVE LOST

IT GETS BETTER

NOW YOU ASK YOURSELF THESE QUESTIONS

LETTING GO

THE ART OF LETTING GO

LETTING GO WITH LOVE

NO REGRETS

LOVE IS UNRETRICTED

Contents

THIS BOOK IS FOR EVERYONE WHO TRIED THEIR BEST

It's sufficient to try. You didn't simply give up or stop. You tried. It doesn't matter how much. It is important that you took all the necessary actions when you had option not to.

Just remember "Good teaches you better, but bad teaches you best."

Foreword

"Do the things that scare you"

Acknowledgements

Dear Readers,

It is with immense joy and gratitude that I welcome you to the pages of my second book, "In my capacity: I love and surrender."

My first book "A strive to find myself" was a voyage into the realm of self-discovery and personal growth—a journey guided by introspection and a desire to offer solace and guidance to those navigating their own paths. Now, in " In my capacity: I love and surrender," I invite you to explore a different facet of my writing—a tapestry woven with imagination, emotion, and the boundless curiosity. Writing has always been my sanctuary—a place where thoughts take flight and emotions find their voice.

As a young writer, I have been inspired by the belief that age is not a barrier to creativity or wisdom. Each word penned is a testament to the capacity of us to perceive the world with clarity and empathy, offering insights that resonate across generations. Through storytelling, I aspire to bridge the gap between perspective and universal truths, inviting readers of all ages to embark on a journey of empathy, understanding, and discovery.

To those who have supported me on this literary odyssey—family, friends, mentors, and readers—I extend my heartfelt gratitude. Your encouragement has fueled my passion and emboldened me to explore new horizons in writing.

May "In my capacity: I love and surrender" inspire you to embrace the wisdom that comes from embracing our true selves and to celebrate the boundless possibilities that await when we dare to dream and to write our own stories.

With gratitude and anticipation,

[Palak Aarohi]

Prologue

Many things happen in our lives that keep burdening us and keep us question everything around, and leave us in dilemma that was it our mistake or theirs, perhaps these are the things that teach us most about our lives and about them too.

Let's dive into a journey of healing, a journey that is different for all of us, yet it is same, a universal journey that unites us all. You will encounter question more than answers in this book, because that's what we are left with, right? QUESTIONS MORE THAN ANSWERS.

In this book, I tried my best to justify each and every question you are having in your head, and trust me when I say this, YOU WILL FEEL BETTER!

Eventually, one day, without any sort of explanation, without any closure, it gets better, it heals, every wound, whether it is brought up by loosing a loved one to death, or being betrayed in friendship or relationship, it eventually gets better, with every passing day.

Through this book, I, the writer of the book, wants to validate what you feel, and be the person you need. Before jumping in the roller coaster ride of healing, I want to let you know that whatever the reason is, trust me when I say this, TIME HEALS!

May this book be a guiding light for you and a companion in your dark moments. I hope you heal soon,

1. STATING YOUR WOUNDS

JUST QUESTIONS

I would like to know why loving you makes me feel ill. Why does it seem like everyday I'm dying a sad, similar death?

Why does it have to kill me inside when you're someone else's, when you are fine without me, when my absence doesn't even hurt you?

Why does it hurt so much that it burns my flesh when you don't love me the way you should, when you walk by me without looking back, or when you don't smile at me the way you always did?

YOU MADE USE OF ME TO FILL THE EMPTINESS THAT WAS INSIDE YOU.

Did you feel scared? That your inner emptiness would destroy you? Leave you feeling even more empty than before? You picked me to fill that vacuum for that reason.

It looked a little more human again because it was my voice that reverberated through your empty walls.

Did I not take your void and put everything I had into it?

That didn't bother me the slightest, but what aches is that you chose to kick me out as soon as the emptiness inside of you stopped eating you up and killing you with every breathe. You were mine from a location that was mine. Why did you give me that place if you weren't?

Why are you happy right now somewhere else? It's unsettling how you transformed me into emptiness I used to fill. Why did you choose me to fill the holes inside you?

I'm so hungry for an answer.

WHY NOT ME

I get it that we weren't lovers. However, we weren't just "friends" either?

Was that not just a small part of it? Why did you smile that was at me if it wasn't?

Why would you care if I was falling apart if we were just friends? Why did you not go? You gave me the impression that you were in love-not only with me.

You gave me hope that I could be chosen by you even though I keep forgetting that I can't be loved. One day, you came to me and said that you wanted someone else-that they are so good that you can't take your eyes off of them, that they would be the perfect person to stand next to you, that you wouldn't mind leaving me for them. You wouldn't mind at all if I went. Were they more attractive? Were there eyes browner? Tell me; I'd want to hear it all.

I know you weren't prepared when it was me, so why did you disobey all of your guidelines when it was someone else?

Tell me, why am I not the one? You chose to break mine and go from me because you didn't want to break their heart or leave them alone. Okay, I get it. <u>But tell me, what about myself?</u>

WHAT UNITES US ALL?

Upon reflection, I see how similar we are.

Both of us don't know each other. We have never met before. But you know what brings us together? Hence, does it make us one?

ANGUISH.

All mine and yours are in pain. It is identical. Strangely, even when people are miles apart, they can experience the same sting, burn, or pain when they witness someone who should be theirs becoming Somone else's. We both experience the same suffering, so you and I are the same.

The anguish is what's bothering me.

THE UNCOMFORTABLE TRUTH

The uncomfortable truth is that if you called, I would still run to you.

I can't resist you, like when I meander into the sweets aisle after swearing off the sugar and discover my favorite chocolate has been restocked. Fuck it, I'll dead with the pain of my broken heart's indulgence later.

I still want the sweetness of you, so I'll eat everything you give me in one sitting. Even though I'm only now starting to heal from the shards of my heart you broke all those months ago, I would fall at your feet once more if it meant you would continue to love me.

NOT EVEN MINE

You are not even mine. You have never been mine.

I'm absolutely at blame. I am at blame because I loved you but you did not. I continued to adore you even after you fell in love with someone else.

I kept onto our memories and your words, Do you realize that I look for you everywhere? You do not. I follow your gaze and attempt to discover myself, but I always fail.

THE SPARK IS GONE

I wonder if the spark will ever reappear. It's gone.

I feel hollow and empty. similar to a blank vessel. which is so in need of holding onto something, someone, yet everything appears to be coming to an end and everyone is gradually disappearing.

How many times have I attempted to better myself and questioned why I always feel so incredibly empty?

Read it out loud

Letting them go was one of the hardest things you could bear, but not as hard as seeing them not want you.

2. ANSWERS TO YOUR QUESTIONS

ANSWER TO ALL THE QUESTIONS

Healing takes time, patience, and self-compassion. Surround yourself with supportive friends and family, engage in activities that bring you joy, and allow yourself to grieve without judgment. Remember, healing isn't linear; it's okay to have good days and bad days.

Firstly, give yourself permission to feel all the emotions that come with the hurt. It's normal to experience sadness, anger, confusion, and even relief or guilt. Each emotion is a part of healing process, allowing you to process the loss and eventually move forward.

We often don't realize how important it is to practice self-compassion and avoid self-blame. Heartbreak is a natural part of life, and it doesn't diminish your worth or values as a person, it is the universal journey that unites us all, treat yourself with the same kindness and understanding that you would offer to a friend going through a similar situation.

Remember, we don't need a closure, the disrespect and the ignorance were the closure. Don't lose your warmth, don't lose your compassion, show them the heart that didn't harden.

They taught you that sometimes the people we love the most are the ones who hurt us the most and how to be compassionate towards them.

They showed you the true strength of the human heart and the depth of sadness that comes from hurting someone you love.

However, love may genuinely endure despite everything.

They showed you that love is never wasted and that we can comprehend when someone breaks our hearts- even if we are in a million pieces- because that is the power of love.

<u>*You will realize then more than ever that leaving was the greatest act of love they have ever committed.*</u>

Make peace with it, Letting go is really not hard, but forcing it is. One of the most significant things you can do for yourself is to avoid taking things personally. Most of the time, someone else's unpleasant acts reflect their own worth rather than yours.

<u>*When your intellect, heart, and soul are in harmony, letting go comes effortlessly. Only the conflict is hard.*</u>

So, how do we find closure within ourselves?

Loving the part of yourself that you have deemed to be "unlovable." Reaching closure entails finishing an internal emotional journey. The person we loved gave us permission to do something, at least in part. They gave us the chance to love and be loved by a part of ourselves that we would not have otherwise given much thought to. Take some time to embrace the parts of yourself you buried to "be more lovable" or "to be enough," and spend time with your embarrassment, guilt, and anguish. You have consistently been lovely and sufficient. Give up trying to be someone you "should be" and just be yourself. Accept and take back every aspect of who you are.

Is there anything as <u>"Unconditional Love"</u>?

The concept of unconditional love is a deeply philosophical and spiritual idea that suggests a love that is given without any conditions or limitations. unconditional love is like loving someone completely, without expecting anything in return. It means accepting someone exactly as they are, flaws and all, and caring for them deeply no matter what happens. It is the kind of love that is not based on conditions or how someone behaves—it is constant and unwavering. Parents often feel this way about their children, where their love remains strong even through tough times. It is a beautiful idea that shows the depth of human connection and compassion.

When their action does not affect your reaction, it is called unconditional love. Unconditional love is when you love someone with your whole heart, no matter what. It means loving them even when they make mistakes or when things are difficult. It's a love that doesn't depend on what the other person does or says—it's there, steady and strong, just because you care about them deeply. It's like having a bond that can weather any storm because it's based on acceptance and understanding. People often aspire to this kind of love because it feels pure and genuine, like a deep connection that goes beyond any conditions or expectations.

Most people don't discover true love until they experience a loss. Since love is unconditional and we can usually only separate after a relationship has "ended," However, in the true detached state, here is where you can explore your heart on a deeper level.

You can unconditionally love someone and still not accept the disrespect. There still are a few conditions in love.

Why is letting go so hard?

Letting go is so hard because the connection was very strong.

Letting go is deeply emotional because it requires us to confront our attachments, fears, and vulnerabilities. It's not just about releasing a physical object or ending a relationship; it's about untangling the complex web of emotions that we've woven around what we're holding onto.

It often involves facing our deepest fears. Fear of loneliness, fear of failure, fear of rejection—the act of letting go can stir up these insecurities because it requires stepping into the unknown.

There's also a profound sense of loss. When we let go, we're mourning not just what was, but also what could have been. We mourn the future we envisioned, the plans we made, and the dreams we held close

to our hearts. It's a grieving process that can be as intense as mourning
the loss of a loved one.

letting go is hard because it requires us to confront our own role in the
situation. It's easy to blame external factors or other people, but letting
go demands a level of self-reflection and acceptance of responsibility. It's
about forgiving ourselves for our mistakes or perceived shortcomings
and finding the strength to move forward.

Why did this happen to you?

"Why did this happen to me?" is a question that generates intense
emotional anguish and a strong sense of vulnerability. When we ask
this question, we are dealing with the shock and disbelief of having
experienced something hurtful or unexpected. It's a heartfelt plea for
understanding the causes of our pain, for making sense of a senseless
circumstance.

In the depths of grief, it's as if the world teamed up against us, sending
us into a void where nothing makes sense. We're left to deal with the
unfairness of it all, wondering what we could have done to deserve this
much pain. It feels like a harsh twist of fate, a punishment imposed
without cause or explanation.

Let me answer this for you;

This happened because it was supposed to be happening, this won't help you ease your pain but this is the ultimate truth, and our entire life an act of accepting and letting go.

*Remember one thing, heartbreak doesn't happen all at once, it happens again and again until you don't move forward. In order come out of this storm as a wise person, you need to go "**through**" it, not "**over**" it or "**past**" it." You need let it hurt you, for it will teach you lessons that perhaps happiness could never. In order to be truly really happy and satisfied with your life you need to experience it all, "the happiness," "the sadness," "the grief," "the loss."*

Don't move on just yet if that's your preference. Letting go requires your whole being, and unless you're totally dedicated to it, there will be a part of you that resists and will try to undermine your efforts at moving on. The conventional "method" of moving on is really forced: hide it, shame it, and this part of you is evil. Space is the ideal location to start. Give yourself permission to feel it and to be human without passing judgement. The issue with shame is that it causes internal conflict because it makes you feel as though you should be experiencing something different from what you are. When people are separated, they are sometimes so devastated that they forget it was their own love in the first place. Never throw away your own heart because it cannot be accepted by another person. This is the gift you offer to yourself—wear your heart on your sleeve and be vulnerable.

FOR THE PEOPLE WHO HAVE LOST

People who have experienced loss understand that you cannot take away another person's love.

People who have lost love understand that when you begin to believe that someone else will take some piece of yourself with them when they walk away, that is when you lose yourself.

People who have lost love understand what it's like to stuff pillows into your empty bed. They are aware of the healing power of accepting it.

The people who have lost love know that you can lose things you never really had, end relationships that never really started. They know that you can mourn people who were never really there at all.

From that extraordinary pain, they learn that someone's love for you isn't lessened or greatened by how much they love someone else.

They know what it's like for there to be strangers in the world who once knew everything about you.

They know you never lose love. They know that what you experience, how you grow, what you take and learn and see and do because of it, is the point.

They are aware that first, you'll be preoccupied with attempting to decide what to do with all of the remaining love.

<u>And they know that you're supposed to give it to yourself.</u>

IT GETS BETTER

It doesn't get better until it does.

Before things get better, they can get worse.

Felling truly loved and joyful can take weeks or even months of grueling days.

Making happiness a constant in your life may not happen right away, but it will eventually.

Your future self is proud of you for surviving to see those days and is aware of what you're going through.

NOW YOU ASK YOURSELF THESE QUESTIONS

- *Who can I turn to for support?*
- *What can I learn from this experience?*
- *What activities or hobbies bring me joy and help me unwind?*
- *Has hate ever made anyone stop mourning?*
- *What role does forgiveness play in this journey?*
- *How can I practice acceptance of the things I cannot change?*
- *Who are the people in my life that lift me up and support me unconditionally?*
- *How can I find moments of joy or beauty in everyday life, despite the pain I am experiencing?*

3. LETTING GO

LETTING GO

You had left the chords a long time ago,

So, I was left with just one knot on myself,

So, I continued to struggle with our ties of attachment.

*I persisted in tugging and pushing in the hopes that you would find a
way to get back to me and our bond would be restored.*

*However, I continued to tie tighter knots on my cords of attachment in
order to force the cords to tighten the bond.*

It began to suffocate me since it was so tight.

I neglected to remember that I can only modify my wires, not yours.

*I had been deluding myself into believing that I am resilient because I
am hanging on.*

*I have decided to cut all of my ties of attachment today since letting go
is the key to strength,*

THE ART OF LETTING GO

I believe that letting go is more than just letting go of the person; it is only one aspect of the healing process. Letting go means accepting that they are not the right person for you and setting them free.

Letting go is the final act of love, it can only happen when your love for them outweighs your urge to talk to them and be with them.

If you've determined that you'll never be able to let go, construct a version of yourself who can. Heal and grow to the point that you are no longer the same person.

*In order to truly and really heal you should feel every iota of your emotion, you need to sit with all the pain. You should understand that it was not your loss, neither it was theirs, when the chapter has ended, you should not try to make them feel bad about it or jealous. You should not try to find someone better **than** them, but you should try to find someone better **for** yourself, precisely as they did.*

<u>The greatest lesson is:</u>

*<u>**The love is mutual, not one sided, that choosing someone at the expense of yourself isn't the most loving thing you can do.**</u>*

*<u>**WALKING AWAY IS!**</u>*

Remember, Love is the cost of experience, not result. The purpose of love is to enjoy what it has to offer, even if it ends one day, rather than necessarily achieving a desired result. NEVER CLOSE YOUR HEART; always keep it open. Because the anguish of not knowing love is far worse than the anguish of experiencing loss.

You need to understand that in this life, you will have to meet every character you are destined to meet, there is no such concept as "Wasted Time", everything you've eventually done has led you to where you are in your life right now, everything you will do will lead you to where you will be in future.

Whether it's a relationship that no longer serves us, a dream that has evolved beyond our reach, or a belief that no longer aligns with our values, letting go demands that we release our grip on the past and open ourselves to new possibilities. This procedure is filled with emotional pain. We are tied not just by our ties to people, objects, or ideas, but also by the memories, hopes, and aspirations that are associated with

them. To let go, we must unwind these emotional knots, the threads of desire and nostalgia that connect us to the past.

letting go challenges our sense of identity.

We often define ourselves by our relationships, achievements, or possessions, and letting go of these can feel like losing a part of ourselves. It forces us to reevaluate our priorities, values, and beliefs, to question who we are without the constructs that once defined us.

The skill of letting go is a profoundly emotional and transforming journey through our inner terrain, deepest fears, and courage. It shows the human spirit's capacity to adapt, grow, and survive in the face of hardship. Finally, it is by letting go that we discover the genuine nature of freedom: the ability to live truly, totally, and in accordance with our greatest goals.

Love is a force that binds us deeply—to people, to memories, to moments that define who we are. Yet, woven within the fabric of love lies an intricate thread of letting go—a paradoxical act of liberation and loss that shapes our journey through life.

To let go with love is to confront the dual nature of attachment: the joy of connection and the pain of separation. It is a profound act of courage, requiring us to release our grip on what once defined us without losing sight of its significance.

The path to letting go with love is not always smooth. It is riddled with the jagged edges of grief, the ache of unfulfilled promises, and the bittersweet realization that some chapters must end for new ones to begin.

In the end, the power of letting go with love lies not in forgetting but in remembering with gratitude.

LETTING GO WITH LOVE

By letting go with love, we learn that endings are not failures, but rather milestones on our road of progress. They teach in us toughness, patience, and the great fact that our capacity for love is limitless. True freedom comes from letting go of the urge for control—a release that allows us to appreciate the beauty of impermanence and value each moment.

NO REGRETS

When I think of you, the only thing that comes to mind is how much I loved you,

Nobody would ever love you as much as I did.

Nobody would desire you as much as I did.

Ask them if they have spent days thinking about how it feels to hear your voice, whether they hunger for you.

Ask them if they will worship you like I did. I have always been a fool, giving too much, but I don't regret it.

I have absolutely no regrets.

You never selected me, yet nobody would love you like I do.

LOVE IS UNRETRICTED

Love is the thing that will set you free; it does not hold you bound to someone.

Love is something that many of us believe we cannot survive without. that need is the cornerstone of love. However, we have convinced ourselves of this deception in order to maintain our relationship.

<u>Love is unrestricted</u>. It is freeing and the only genuine solution we have when we have a strong emotional attachment to someone.

In its purest form, love is also detached. It's embracing something for what it is, not for what you wish it to be.

RIGHT PERSON, WRONG TIME

One of the usual sensations we get during separation is "right person, wrong time," but in reality, it all comes down to perception. Perhaps they are the wrong person at the perfect moment. Their meeting was necessary for a purpose.

We can finally break free from some imagined future and live out the story we were destined to live once we accept this.

HEART OF SAPPHIRE

You may think things like "I loved them more than I loved anyone, I never knew I could love someone so much, I'll never love someone that much again" when you are healing from a person. <u>It is crucial to understand that you are the one who is capable of loving that person; it is not something they gave you. You were a lover from the beginning and had a great capacity for love. It doesn't go away just because they're gone. They provided you with a space to express your love, but they did not grant you the ability to love. Give no credit to anyone else for your ability to love deeply; that was and still is you.</u>

FINAL ACT OF LOVE

When stars collide it is transformed into a supernova being most beautiful than ever, when we think we are breaking maybe God is trying to transform us into supernova, which is our most beautiful self.

This journey of healing is yours, it is all yours, people will meet you at every corner, very rare people will walk with to from corner to corner but not all the time, their will come a time where you have to sit with yourself, just you and no one, People can advise you, guide you, show you the way but no one will walk it for you, Only you and you can pull yourself out of the abyss.

<u>In reality, what we're doing when we commit to the "final act of love" is returning to ourselves. to make our own decisions once more. To ultimately understand that everything has always been within of you, you must lose "everything" that is outside of you. How much "love" must you lose before you realize it's coming from yourself at the end? All you have to do is look in the mirror and freely acknowledge that your soulmate, your other half, has been waiting for you to see them at last.</u>

So, yes, endings are beginnings too. They are not just the closing of a chapter, but the opening of a

new one—one filled with possibility, growth, and self-discovery. They remind us that even in our darkest moments, there is always light on the horizon, waiting to guide us forward on our journey of love.

<u>ENDINGS ARE BEGINNINGS TOO, SOMEONE ELSE'S ENDING IN YOUR LIFE IS YOUR BEGINNING IN YOUR LIFE.</u>

<u>You are supposed to give all that love to yourself!</u>

Are you ready for it?

Dear Reader,

I hope this message finds you well and immersed in the pages of my book. <u>As the author, I feel compelled to clarify that the story within these chapters is not based on any events from my personal life</u>. The theme explored—particularly the art of letting go has always been in my mind.

The concept of letting go has always fascinated me. It's a universal experience that touches each of us in unique ways, yet it's something we all must confront at some point in our lives. Through this book, I aimed to delve into the complexities of releasing attachments, navigating through emotional turmoil, and ultimately finding inner peace and resilience.

I hope that as you read these pages, you find solace and inspiration in the exploration of letting go. May this book serve as a companion on your own journey of self-discovery and healing.

Thank you for joining me on this literary exploration. Your support means the world to me.

Warm regards,

[Palak Aarohi]

A Note To Reader

Dear valued reader,

Thank you all for purchasing this book. I hope it will help you to see the idea of love, loss and letting go from a totally different perspective.

It will be a great pleasure for me reading your reviews on

<u>connectpalakaarohi@gmail.com</u>

9 798889 498510 7